PATRIARCHY AND PUB CULTURE

A

PATRIARCHY

PUB CULTURE

VALERIE HEY

TAVISTOCK PUBLICATIONS
LONDON AND NEW YORK

First published in 1986 by
Tavistock Publications Ltd
11 New Fetter Lane, London EC4P 4EE

© 1986 Valerie Hey

Typeset by AKM Associates (UK) Ltd, Southall, Greater London

Printed in Great Britain

British Library Cataloguing in Publication Data
Hey, Valerie
    Patriarchy and pub culture. — (Social
    science paperbacks; no. 323)
    1. Hotels, taverns, etc. — Social aspects
    — Great Britain
    I.Title   II. Series
    306.4'8   GT3843

ISBN 0-422-60260-4

CONTENTS

ACKNOWLEDGEMENTS

I've been drinking in pubs since I was seventeen and I've been a feminist since I was twenty-four but it wasn't until 1982 that I had the opportunity to understand the first activity in the context of the second. For their encouragement of my writing on the Women's Studies course at Kent (for which the first draft of this text was presented as my MA dissertation), I'd like to thank Mary Evans and Jeffrey Weeks. My thanks also go to the following: for housing me during summer, autumn, and winter 1982 and providing unequalled hospitality, the Smith household; for her wonderful support at that time and since, my particular friend Helly Langley; for his commitment to me and to this project, Guido Casale. And lastly, to Laura Grace, who came along after the dissertation and before the book.

INTRODUCTION

He's got it right!

If I were to cite my nomination for the most oppressive television advertisement it would be the following. Enter young woman into the lounge bar of a pub; we see her from the point of view of two young males at the bar. She arranges a stool, purchases a drink and places it on the table, and leaves. Young males and the viewer remain puzzled. She returns assisting her 'boyfriend', whose leg is in plaster, and props his leg on to the stool, serving him his drink. Ah . . . all is explained, as the three men – nudge, nudge, wink, wink – appreciate her gesture of solicitude. 'He's got it right!' in more ways than one. This male collusion does not threaten one man's 'right' to his attractive 'possession'; in fact, it enhances the status of the 'owner', who is tacitly complimented on 'owning' a woman who is manifestly servile.

At a general level, it is possible to read this narrative as confirming several related pub practices, as well: namely, that the only legitimate way a woman can buy a man a drink is if he is physically incapable of buying it himself and that 'public' houses are male 'playgrounds' to which women are 'invited' on special terms. The first reaction of the men at the bar to the lone woman was one of predatory curiosity. This aggressive, self-conscious 'interest' ends only when her presence is explained by her 'boyfriend's' injury.

The impact of this advertisement is assured because we are *not* free to read it any other way. The viewer inevitably sees it from the patriarchal point of view. We are all implicated in the meanings which construct *us*. We, as well as the 'lads' are surprised about her singularity in this territory. Her sexuality is represented by the obligatory outfit of dermis-tight denims, *décolleté* blouse, and high heels. The opposition between her sexuality and the 'men-only' ethos of the pub sets up groups of anti-feminist meanings, which we make at the same time as we reject them. We think her 'on the prowl', 'on the loose', or even 'on the game'. Unaccompanied and unexplained, we place her in all these categories because there exists in popular culture and practice a conception that pubs for the most part are male enclaves and that individual women who enter them are therefore 'after only one thing'.

It will be the purpose of this book to provide a more detailed investigation of this and other social interpretations that attach to this particular social institution. My purpose will be to add to our political understanding about male behaviour as expressed in the 'local' and to offer some clues as to why women's relation to this particular expression of visible pleasure and leisure is, to put it mildly, far more problematic.

Male ability to command and control a space seems to be one of the first lessons of social learning. Shirley Ardener notes, in another context, that any space where men are present in large numbers becomes designated as 'public' and, at the same time, ironically, 'out of bounds for women' (Ardener 1978:32). Observe any school playground: the physical space carved out by the vigorous activities of young males literally pushes young females to the edges. Football takes up much more room than skipping. The securing of territory and the retention of it by physical/verbal means is a

4

recurrent symbol and expression of male dominance and female subordination. Women have only to think here of the 'no-go' areas of the street after dark as the most dramatic and frightening instance of male terrorism. At a less violent level, male segregation is expressed to show the personal self-sufficiency of the speaker in the discourse of space and distance: 'You didn't need to get too heavily into sex or pulling chicks, or sorts as they were called. . . . *Women were just the people who were dancing over in the corner by the speakers'* (quoted in McRobbie 1980:43; my emphasis).

It is a repeated finding of the following research that men seem unable to express self-sufficiency except in terms of abuse and contempt, the rhetoric and realities of which permeate both their pub cultures and their subcultures.

I originally wanted to understand the male domain of recreational public drinking because of several personal encounters, visits to pubs which were disturbing. I make no claim to be uniquely qualified to 'theorize' or make sense of these experiences. I know that my experience of harassment is, in fact, common and it is my desire to deal with my past humiliation and offer some clues as to the reasons for my treatment that prompt me to construct a view of the gender relations of pubs. I don't think that male and female inter-actions spontaneously erupt, like volcanoes; what happens to men and to women in pubs is explicable in terms of patriarchal social relations. When I started thinking about pub politics, however, I had only a very unwieldy and simplistic notion of male power/female oppression as a starting point. The aim of this account is to make more complex our understanding of male practice and female responses.

To provide the texture to the process, I will begin with two semi-literary versions of my visits to the 'male domain':

Do you come here often?
SCENE ONE – A PROVINCIAL PUB

I plan to meet a male friend after an evening out. I remember. He forgets. I'm stranded like a liberal in the White House. A stranger, unwelcome. I receive unwelcome advances of the quasi-drunken kind. Close encounters. I try to keep cool and sophisticated. I fail. Tell him to blankety-blank. The other customers stare at *me*. How dare I spoil the fun! I leave, humiliated and irate.[1]

A woman's right to booze?
SCENE TWO – A METROPOLITAN PUB

A Constituency Labour Party's Women's Section meeting. Theme: A woman's right to work. After the meeting, two groups of women occupy two separate rooms in the local pub. Group A consists of three women, including myself. Group B consists of nine women. For reasons that will appear obvious later, I'll call Group A the 'theorists' and Group B the 'activists'.

'The "theorists" sit down. Within five minutes, one comprehensively drunken man moves across and proceeds to gesture behind my back. He then commences a game called "Tell us your names". Two of the "theorists" concede this familiarity; I don't and he accuses me of being "unfriendly". He returns to his circulating gestures. One of my group tells him to stop. I tell him to go. I try to involve his companions, whose social responsibility goes only so far as to drink his drink. One of them turns on me and says that I'm "a troublemaker, one of those psychologists". A woman in the group restrains him. He stands up over me. He sits down. The "rambler" continues. I refuse to contribute. He starts waving a finger in my face. I crack and snap that "if he doesn't put away his finger . . . I'll . . . etc., etc." His companions leave and go outside. He falls into their space and stops pestering us. A victory? I am emotionally drained, my "quiet" drink has become a battle of nerves. I'm left reflecting with my women friends on the violence that our lack of compliance incited. We feel sickened. We leave at closing time and tell the others about our story and they tell us theirs.'

'The "activists" sit down in the darts bar. One man was heard to say, as they entered, "I'll soon get rid of this lot!" He persists in abusing them all in general and one woman in particular. She dresses in a "non-feminine" way. (She has been entertaining us all at the meeting with her songs.) He accuses them of being lesbians when they want to continue talking to each other instead of to him and his mates. The aggression escalates, the "singer" calculates how to cope with his insults. She has trained in one of the martial arts but the darts bar is too small and crowded. Verbal retaliation, as Liz Stanley found out in her research on dealing with dirty phone calls (Stanley 1982), merely implicates women in situations controlled by men and can be wilfully misread by men as "playing hard to get". So, looking at his nearly empty glass and her nearly full one, she pours her drink all over him. He's saturated and shocked. His retaliation is to throw his dregs on her, and leave. She only gets a little wet. The rest of the group are astonished at her composure and come to tell us about their evening.

We can hardly credit that two separate groups of women simultaneously incur so much resentment and hostility in the space of one pub and forty-five minutes. We decide that our next meeting has to be about sexual harassment!'

In the light of the above and other evidence, it is hardly surprising that women have not been attracted to drinking in pubs, let alone thinking and writing about them. This book is one small contribution to this need, since I think we can learn a great deal from this social organism, rather along the lines of Liz Stanley's sub-title to her paper: 'Why men oppress women; or how experiences of sexism can tell us interesting and useful things about women's liberation'. What *is* surprising, however, is the dearth of work by men on this prime site of 'male enjoyment'. Given that 'popping out for a quick one' / 'taking the dog for a walk' / 'whetting the whistle' is one of the most popular male recreational activities, what is it that has prevented men from taking this institution seriously?

Is it not the fact that, as Georg Simmel remarked: 'Man's position of power does not only assure his relative superiority over the woman, but it assures that his standards become generalized as generically human standards' (quoted in Pearson 1982: 2)? Pearson argues that if this is the case 'not only have women been hidden, but the maleness of men has been hidden from sociological enquiry, and it is past time that "he" was brought into the light of day'.

By bringing 'him' into the light of day, I hope to contribute to the process begun by Ann Whitehead (1976), whose important and neglected study 'Sexual Antagonism in Herefordshire', provides added motivation to persist in taking 'the boys' seriously.

Consequently, what I have pieced together is drawn from many fields of knowledge and is a highly speculative account of the political relations of men and women as acted out inside the pub. Apart from Ann Whitehead's ethnographic study I have used two principal socio-historical studies: Brian Harrison's work on Victorian pubs (1971, especially Chapters 1, 2, 14 and 16; 1973) and Mass Observation's sociological investigation into 'Worktown's' pubs, edited by Tom Harrisson (1943). In addition I have utilized some elements of Diana Leonard's (1980) work on marriage in a Swansea community, especially pages 147–52 on 'stag' and 'hen' parties, where she refers to the cultural differences in the ways women and men make the transition from the single to the married state. Roger Smith (1976) consolidated my early views on pubs and he has some interesting and pertinent things to say about the cultural/political and personal advantages men obtain from their access to informal Fleet Street folk – knowledge represented in the street's many pubs.

Allied to providing a synthesis of these 'borrowings', I want to see how some anthropological categories fit the English public-house culture: for example, I'm intrigued by the concept of public/private (already alluded to) as developed by Michelle Rosaldo (1974) and I wonder how far men's occupation of pubs and special rooms within them counts as a distancing strategy, a way to manipulate their social absence from or presence with their intimates of the same and the other sex.[2]

Finally, this book will be an attempt to amplify the notion of 'unbonding' as a male taboo, for it seems to me that this concept, introduced by Stoltenberg, is a very useful orientation point in getting our bearings before we open the pub door:

'Under patriarchy, the cultural norm of human identity is by definition – masculinity. And under patriarchy the cultural norm of male identity consists in power, prestige, privilege and prerogative as over and against the gender class women.... Male bonding is institutionalized learned behavior whereby men recognize and reinforce one another's bona fide membership in the male gender class ... male bonding is how men learn from each other that they are entitled under patriarchy to power in the culture. Male bonding is how men get that power and male bonding is how it is kept. Therefore men enforce a taboo against unbonding.'   (Quoted in Brake 1980:151)

Notes

1 See Hey (1980) for a fuller account of this experience.
2 'Distance permits men to manipulate their social environment, to stand apart from intimate interaction, to control it as they wish.... Because men can be separate they can be sacred and by avoiding certain sorts of intimacy and unmediated involvement they can develop an image and mantle of integrity and worth' (Rosaldo and Lamphere 1974:27). Rosaldo usefully compares this luxurious (if problematic) detachment with the female/child attachment: 'Men have no single commitment as enduring, time-consuming and emotionally compelling, as close to seeming necessary and natural as the relation of a woman to her infant child' (Rosaldo and Lamphere 1974:24).

A masculine republic in every street

Victorian public houses appear to have been all things to all men. For their clientele, they provided unrivalled recreational facilities at affordable prices to groups whose working life was so tightly meshed into the wheels of a developing capitalist economy that 'time off' became more and more squeezed out of the working day as the needs of Capital structured the rhythms of working people's lives.[1]

In such a bleak landscape of unremitting labour the Victorian pub must have seemed like an overnight stop-over, half-way to paradise. Not only did the pubs provide drinks whose alcoholic strength was considerably higher than our strongest contemporary brews, they also provided ample social and recreational opportunities in warm, well-lit, and comfortable buildings. Customers had access to newspapers, betting games, cock fighting arenas, political meeting places, debating societies, sporting venues, and transport centres all in the context of company, social networks, and street and community gossip. Pubs formed a focal point for the vigorous and tumultuous street life so despised and feared by the 'respectable' temperance campaigners of the era.

For these – the majority – unable to afford more cultural pursuits, living in a society starved of leisure, the attractions of the Victorian pub must have been immense. As Harrison enthusiastically remarks,

> 'the extravagant and crowded atmosphere of the pub helped Victorian publicans to pursue their important recreational role. *Imagine the dram shop's impact on a tired and working man fleeing from his drab home, nagging wife or landlady, and crying children.*   (Harrison 1971:171; my emphasis)

One might add, to parody Mary McIntosh, that 'pub recreation is there for the needs of the tired and working man, no one asks how the tired and working woman manages'.[2]

It will be the purpose of my deconstruction of Harrison's text to ask precisely that last question. For what emerges from his study is a very clear pattern of gender differentiation within and without this particular social space, and what he both records and evades forms a paradigm of male domination made possible by female exclusion, control, and oppression. All the chief strategies that he sees and excuses are prefigurations of male behaviour in other historical moments, so that he produces an account of a historically specific but not historically unique record of patriarchal 'pleasure'.

It may be argued that Harrison's concerns lie with measuring the balance of social forces for and against temperance and that of necessity his interest is centred on describing and analysing the class loyalties and interests that were provoked over the struggle to maintain access to pleasurable, companionable drinking. Given that the main subject of his work is class relations, one might well concede this emphasis. Indeed, any account of the development of pubs and resistance to them that ignored class would hardly be intelligible.

Not all social phenomena are explicable by nor reducible to class relations, however, and this over-reliance on material relations between groups as constituting the historical dynamic means that simultaneously women's relation to the pub is recognized as different but this difference is neither fully encountered, explained, nor taken seriously. In fact, Harrison performs a series of fairly dextrous moves to hold certain important truths/interpretations of women's position at a distance.

Throughout his narrative there is a tension between his confident espousal of the 'class conflict' level of analysis and his continuing discovery of a very awkward group (female persons) who keep cropping up outside of that level of explanation. Not only do they evade the materialist net on occasion, there is a major discrepancy in their 'rights to leisure' in the first instance. It has already been remarked that in Victorian times the working classes met leisure as frequently as the Tory government meets the TUC but even within such brief periods of free time women's time off or absence from the home was less than men's – in fact, that is an understatement! We are not in a position to construct accurate statistics about female leisure patterns in Victorian society but we can critically highlight the assumptions of the historians of that period, who fail adequately to explain why the Victorian pub became 'a masculine republic in every street'.

Something less innocent is going on in Harrison's case than mere explanatory shortcomings, however, since he is actively engaged in presenting rationalizations for the gender relations that he on the one hand acknowledges and on the other hand neutralizes. Halfway through his paper on pubs he remarks:

> 'To a large extent the pub was a centre of male recreation and the temperance movement liked to see itself as defending helpless women and children against male selfishness.'   (Harrison 1973:174)

Plate 1.1 Temperance and intemperance at home. *British & Foreign Temperance Intelligencer*, 21 March, 1840, p. 89.
(The British Library)

This might well have been the case but it is also possible that working women may have been attracted to the temperance movements for their own reasons; i.e. they may have wished to secure more of their husbands' company and support (both emotional and financial). Harrison doesn't acknowledge this as a possibility. After all, women had little to lose in a social arrangement where, because of their domestic commitments, they were temperate by necessity.

Harrison's research uncovers ample evidence that Victorian working-class women both resented and challenged the power of the pub over their men and their income. And the price they paid in physical violence is well documented, though there is a familiar shifting of blame onto the female that will be noted in my re-interpretation of Harrison's history in Chapter 2. See, for example, this instance:

'To make matters worse, drunken husbands were often *stung* by the wife's silent or open reproach into the wife-beating for which English men were notorious abroad.'

(Harrison 1971:47; my emphasis)

Note the passive voice of the verb, suggesting an action *committed by the wife on the husband*. N.F. Charrington was so appalled by one incident of male brutality that he witnessed that his conversion to teetotalism was permanent and meant a rejection of his family's fortune and a life devoted to charitable work in the East End (reported in Harrison 1973:169). Similarly powerful scenes are noted in *Drink and the Victorians*:

'Drinking places on paydays were besieged by wives desparately anxious to feed and clothe the family; many married couples fought over the wage packet, and many wives were kept ignorant of its contents.'   (Harrison 1971:46)

The battle over resources was particularly acute for women with large families and there is evidence that a man's drinks expenditure probably *increased* with the size of his family (Harrison 1971:46).

Great play is made in Harrison's narrative of the miserable living conditions enjoined on working-class people by their exploitation by Capitalism and landlordism. We are told that the home was still 'oftener a place to fly FROM than to fly TO' (1971:46) and we are specifically informed that 'the working *man's* home was often cold, uncomfortable and noisy; he and his wife lived at too close quarters' (1971:46). In such remarks we can observe the presumption of a male right of passage, a right to an exit out of the discomfort and to an ability to purchase comforts at the collective level which a man's income couldn't command on the personal. Even Harrison has to recognize this male selfishness:

'The nineteenth century drinking place, like the twentieth century expense account, encouraged men to enjoy better living standards than their wives.'   (Harrison 1971:46)

I would go further and say that the pub, unlike the expense account, enabled (and enables) men to enjoy better living standards *at the expense of their wives*. This shift in emphasis marks my difference from Harrison and I want to enlarge on this discord by examining his text in detail for his methods of coping with 'male selfishness'.

I have already commented on the extent to which his over-concentration on class relations distorts the historical reconstruction. Gender relations are, as a consequence, underplayed and there is no serious or satisfactory investigation of the extent to which female and male interests might be in contradiction.

Several results are produced by this failure to politicize gender differences and they follow from an inadequate recognition that male/female relations are ideologically, socially, and economically structured in terms of dominance and subordination. Harrison's excuse of male privilege is, in essence, to rely upon 'common sense', naturalized notions of femininity versus masculinity as acted out in a timeless 'battle of the sexes'.

Let us examine his arguments in some detail.[3] First, he suggests that dominant women 'created' drunken, absent husbands, citing current music-hall songs of the era as evidence, with their lyrics concerning the strident 'missus'. Secondly, he alleges that the existence of 'masculine republics limited potential sources of conflict and ensured that at least some house-proud women had no rivals in the home'. It follows from his first point that women are better off subordinate since dominant women 'provoke' male vengeance in the form of alcoholism, which can be then blamed back onto women.

Harrison's second point, part of what he sees as a 'differentiation of social function' is a classic rationalization of the sexual division of labour. A woman's prime responsibility for servicing a household with her unpaid domestic labour is repackaged as a privilege and male absence is viewed as a welcome bonus to be sanctioned enthusiastically, enabling an unfettered indulgence in housework. There is, of course, no way of knowing whether some Victorian working women acted in this stereotypical way but the fact that Harrison utilizes this cosy model of functionally harmonious marital roles is interesting. It works like a veil to cover the social realities that his account had already specified: women's poverty and desperation seem more the order of the day than this confected cosy domesticity.

Harrison's third strategy is the familiar rhetoric of 'different but equal', in which we are told that women, though restricted to the home, had their own 'scene' to compensate them: 'If women were excluded from the public house they had their own recreation in "stair-head" drinking clubs, chapel life and local gossip.'

Apart from simply commenting that men could enter this world too, whereas the same could not be said of women's access to public drinking, all the above social activities (apart from chapel-going) are domestically based. I am not proposing to judge the relative social benefits extracted by each sex from their sex-segregated options but it seems evident that if women are at home they never really have 'time off' – their availability to children is assured. Any pleasure to be gained from other sources is a diluted experience if it always takes place in the context of being responsible for childcare as well.

I am not suggesting that women did not make adult friends in these 'stair-head' social occasions but such liaisons are not equivalent to the opportunities men enjoyed to relax and experience social cohesion and solidarity, a point Harrison himself makes in an oblique reference to what he terms women's 'apolitical' inclinations. (I will return to this concept later, since it is one of the crucial effects and causes of patriarchal privilege.)

Fourth, and allied to his attempt to construct women as causal factors cited earlier, Harrison resorts to accusations of female slovenliness:

'In other cases the home suffered from the wife's laziness or ignorance. By offering her outside employment, industrialization deprived her of time and energy for housework, and even caused a reversal of roles in which wives became wage earners and husbands domestic drudges.'

Whilst noting his description of household labour as drudgery, when it is done by men, though he regards it as creatively essential for women to undertake, we cannot let this set of opinions stand as social fact. What seems to be at issue, apart from women's basic unreliability, is a resentment of Capitalist power to distract women away from their 'natural' affinity to drudgery.

To clinch his apologia for male monopolization of pubs, Harrison resorts to an old device, that of accusing women of the same vice from which he is exculpating men. He paints a lurid picture of female alcoholism. In a depiction that is unsupported by any evidence, he declares that 'sometimes husbands far from selfishly squandering the family income, came home to find that their wives had drunk away the furniture'. This construction of the female alcoholic is deployed later in his book when he is writing on the phenomena of so-called 'underemployment'.

'Even today the under-employed middle class housewife is more likely than fully employed members of society to become an alcoholic; frequent were the nineteenth-century tales of concealed intemperance above stairs.'

(Harrison 1971:305)

Apart from the ludicrous and statistically unsupportable description of middle-class housewives as both 'under-employed' (he's obviously never been involved in the care of children and domestic labour!) and as actually *outnumbering* the 'fully employed' (which I take as a coded way of describing men) in their predisposition to alcoholism, we are witnessing a very clear attempt to legitimize male behaviour by suggesting it constitutes only a *half* of the full picture. It is granted that men like their beer but we are told of female self-indulgence to 'balance' the social reality.

To dramatize the reservations I have about Harrison's whole tone on Victorian social drinking patterns, I'd like to quote his closing remarks on the issue. We are told that 'the picture is therefore complex, and even where, by modern standards – male selfishness did exist, *there were good reasons for it*' (my emphasis). Within the terms of the argument that I've outlined, it becomes quite clear that women and women's behaviour are the constructed 'good reasons'. These nagging harridans whose alleged dominance, slovenliness, fastidiousness, and alcoholism are used to 'explain' a male resort to masculine company and alcohol. Male power, as manifested in their violence, control of time and money, their absence and availability, remains the hidden sub-text of such patriarchal discourse, and it is with this that the rest of this book will be concerned.

Notes

1 This chapter is a response to Brian Harrison's work on Victorian drinking and the struggles of the 'respectable' classes against male 'enjoyment' of alcoholic drinks (1971,1973).
2 Mary McIntosh's essay (1978) provided a model for my own interpretation of Harrison's reading of Victorian history.
3 All the following quotations and paraphrased lines of argument are to be found in Harrison (1971:46–7), unless otherwise indicated.

2

Consuming passions:
Victorian views on virility
and female sexuality

If we compare two photographs from *Drink and the Victorians* (Harrison 1971) we find some telling differences that visualize the content of this chapter. I am referring to the pictures of Solomon King and Margaret Wilson; on pages 26 and 27. Solomon King sits, with hands on his knees with his eyes looking past us into the mid-distance. His expression is one of a resigned defiance; an unapologetic and uncompromising sense of himself and his position. Margaret Wilson's picture is much more poignant. She clutches her hands nervously across her lap. Her head is bowed in a posture of dejection, shame, and defeat. Her eyes do not seek ours, they are concentrated at a point on the floor.

Given that their 'careers' seem roughly comparable, how are we to explain their contrasting demeanours? It is my belief that the answer to this question does not lie in details of their personal biographies but in the cultural expectations of Victorian society, ideologies of appropriate masculinity and femininity that have continuing relevance to modern notions of male/female behaviour.

Working-class notions of masculinity were very much grounded in 'drinking deeply', which was both a sign and an expression of one's virility. There were complex and secret customs, particularly in the skilled crafts, concerning the

Plate 2.1 Solomon King, arrested for drunkenness, at Dunstable, 1866. *Register of Prisoners in Bedford County Gaol*, p. 70. (Bedford County Record Office)

Plate 2.2 Margaret Wilson, frequently arrested for drunkenness. *Register of Prisoners in Bedford County Gaol*, p. 124. (Bedford County Record Office)

'rites of passage' from apprenticeship to master craftsman, which all depended on alcohol consumption. 'Working men marked their son's maturity by making them publicly drunk at a "rearing" '(Harrison 1971:39).

It was widely believed, too, that beer was an essential source of energy, particularly relevant to men in strenuous physical occupations (Harrison 1971:39). Closely allied to its renewing facilities, alcohol was claimed as an aphrodisiac, with stout and oysters particularly recommended.[1] Agricultural labourers held on to the ancient belief that it was impossible to glean the harvest without 'harvest beer'. And, as Harrison remarks:

> 'nor were these beliefs entirely unfounded though intoxicants were no better than food for providing energy, their stimulating effects could temporarily dull the fatigue resulting from long hours and hard labour.'
>
> (Harrison 1971:39)

The ideology of increased physical potency encouraged men to consume and the ability to 'take one's ale' became imprinted as a mark of masculinity – a distinction that was not confined to the male proletariat. Lord Randolph Churchill once declared that 'the aristocracy and the working class are united in the indissoluble bands of a common immorality' (quoted in Harrison 1973:174), which not only referenced their joint interest in drinking but also indicated their similar 'consumption' of prostitutes in drinking places that developed a sideline in supplying locations for paid sex. Some pubs were brothels, others provided non-sexual services to their customers. I have already hinted at the range of facilities the average man could have enjoyed at his local pub.[2]

I shall look here at the specific institution of prostitution as it became identified with certain pubs, since it shows the working of both ideology and male practice on material realities. This historical purpose is crucial to modern injunctions operating to keep pubs predominantly male – I would argue that it ideologically 'contaminates' women who work in or drink in pubs. (See later in this chapter and Chapter 3 for the development of this argument.) This may seem like a long route away from the photographs but I hope to show how Victorian pub cultures both reflected and created gender relations that are glimpsed in those two expressions.

To support this argument, I'd like to return to the concept of a 'masculine republic' and to put this descriptive phrase in context.

In the transition from pre-industrial to post-industrial Britain, traditional family networks seem to have been disrupted, throwing to the surface a group of individuals whose needs were not met by the new social arrangements in which they found themselves. Harrison evokes a constituency of single males whose displacement from more nurturant rural economies presented opportunities for other social structures to meet the 'shortfall'. Into this identification of 'need' he inserts the public house and its potentialities. He describes the relations between the economy and its clients thus:

'If working men were unemployed, in lodgings, "flitting" from one house to another, or trapped in the bachelor trades, their dependence on the publican was complete.'
(Harrison 1973:172)

It is this social and economic milieu that provides the starting point for a discussion of the publican's role in supplying prostitutes to the 'bachelor' clients. It is important

29

to state from the beginning of this section that the whole trade in female sexuality to meet the demands of male sexuality was structured in terms of male demand/female supply. It was male sexual 'urges' that were recognized as 'needing' satisfaction; female sexuality was not thought of in terms of activity and desire but merely of consumption.

Harrison presents a very clear description of a large group of allegedly frustrated males whose sexual urges were recognized and legitimized in the 'solution' of prostitution. This sexual servicing function of a public house interests me because I think that this particular historical role permeates popular, modern consciousness in a way I recognize but cannot fully explain. To suggest the connections between a historical legacy and current experience, I'd propose that it is still practically impossible for single women to consume pints of beer in a pub without their activity being read as a sexually deviant or defiant action. I would like to meet the woman who can unselfconsciously enter a strange public house alone. It is one of the consequences of a patriarchal control of female sexuality that we are prevented from 'popping into the local' for a social drink, unaccompanied.

Historically, working-class pubs in their role as 'female substitutes' – offering plentitude, availability, warmth, food, and companionship, a servicing of male needs – were effective purveyors of available female sexuality to a 'bachelor' class. The 'bachelors' were created by the market place via a wide ranging set of regulations; for example, certain working men were debarred from marriage until an appropriate age. In addition, a large group of servicemen were regulated into singularity, being discouraged from marriage by Government statutes. The publican's response to such a captive audience was typically entrepreneurial:

'Publicans helped to recruit, to billet and to entertain the armed forces. Government policy by discouraging service-men from marrying, inevitably encouraged publicans in garrison towns and seaports to provide prostitutes and to devour the savings which servicemen accumulated over-seas.'   (Harrison 1973:172)

It is significant to record that it is the exercise and expression of male sexuality that is the identified 'problem'. It is assumed that there is a naturalistic alliance between the publican and the prostitute concerning the satisfaction of these 'inevitable' male sexual needs.

'The alliance between publican and prostitute was natural: the publican presided over a meeting place where human relations of all kinds were established, sold a powerful solvent of barriers between individuals, and was generally associated with recreational gaiety. His house was as suitable a "house of call" for prostitutes as for any other trade'.   (Harrison 1971:50)

As already intimated, the response to this identified 'lack' was a flurry of free-trade initiatives. Pub-based prostitution was deliberately created and encouraged in garrison towns with their captive, male, segregated populations. Pub densities were higher in garrison towns and there was a significantly higher number of public houses clustered around barracks. Harrison (1971) draws attention to the preponderance of pubs outside the Wellington and Knightsbridge Barracks and provides ample evidence of the social service pubs performed in making good the alleged 'lacks' of servicemen's lives. Publicans in Aldershot, apparently anxious to maintain their trade in supplying prostitutes, employed surgeons to ensure that women in their houses were certified clean. This precautionary move was made well before the legislated intervention of the Contagious Diseases Act (Harrison 1971:332).

There was a hierarchy of response to the 'problem' of male celibacy. Upper-echelon prostitutes would be in a position to rent adjoining property from a landlord 'on the understanding that customers would be collected only in his taproom'. 'Lower'-class prostitutes merely rented rooms on his premises (Harrison 1971:332).[3] From inside the working-class male culture, therefore, came positive encouragement to men to drink in quantity and satisfy their sexual appetites. Indeed it was incumbent on men to do so, to show the necessary virility.[4]

If we compare this set of cultural expectations with Victorian notions of appropriate female behaviour, we can begin to see why Solomon King looks past us while Margaret Wilson can't face us. I think the crux of the difference is the fear of female sexuality and the almost universal, trans-historical, trans-class, and cross-race need of men to control its expression on terms that they establish.

In Victorian society there was a general ideology of female discretion and domestic 'privacy'. Women were encouraged to be self-denying, pleasure-giving and not pleasure-taking, except as far as their homes, husbands, and children provided. Originating in the leisured and propertied social classes, this ideology permeated other aspiring social strata and the ability to 'keep a wife at home' became one of the marks of 'respectability' enjoined on the working classes although, if it was to some extent taken up by the more prosperous elements, it could never be the common practice of all.[5] However, this cultural climate set the tone for male views on female sexuality, even if in practice economic necessity meant that women worked outside the home as well as within it in a great many households.

Closely associated with notions of female purity/pollution (see Douglas 1966) was an insistence on female self-control. At the same time that men of the working classes were incited to indulge their 'passions', women of the same class became increasingly subjected to supervision of their enjoyment.

In the popular imagination, drunkenness in women equated with sexually improper conduct in a way that rendered women who drank beneath contempt. Their lack of self-restraint was viewed as far more threatening and morally offensive than the equivalent male action. (This is still true today. The representation of the male alcoholic in films is sympathetic, and there is usually a nurturant female to pick him out of the gutter. No such kindliness surrounds the female 'lush'.) Margaret Wilson had far more to contend with than Solomon King; because of her gender, she had no peer group to absorb and sustain her activities.

This is not to suggest that women were totally compliant and privatized, confined to their homes, leaving pubs to the men. There is, of course, evidence of women's presence in pubs but we should note that their relation to this institution was ambivalent and tangential and their 'toleration' as customers found expression in their physical occupation of quiet, unobtrusive, and separated bars. We are told that 'women gossiped and drank in little one-sex groups in the *"private"* bars' (Girouard 1975:11). Out of sight, out of mind? Almost as if their visibility reminded men that they too had a 'right to leisure' – a situation that men reacted to with a hostility that made women feel more comfortable in a subculture pub culture.[6] Further, evidence to the Peel Commission quoted in Girouard (1975) suggests that these secluded little bars were popular with women because their 'husbands couldn't see them'; it was physically possible to slip into and out of the building without drawing too much attention to oneself.

Interestingly enough, there is another reference to the Victorian use of 'small bars' in Girouard's book that brings together many of the themes that I have been discussing in this chapter. (I leave the sexist language as indicative of the male double-standard.) He avers:

'Small bars may on occasion have been used for illicit sex but it was certainly not their only use. They were extremely popular with women on their own as well as accompanied by men, and respectable women as well as, probably more than, tarts.'   (Girouard 1975:11)

This extract neatly summarizes the major themes of this chapter, for what we read here is an expression of the patriarchal double-standard and its effect on women. Namely, that women's sexuality and behaviour is controlled by the ability of men to designate 'deviant' women as prostitutes and, therefore, non-respectable. Any lone woman in a pub can be placed in the 'non-respectable' category for the historical reason that the only women who entered pubs openly *were* prostitutes, whose services were demanded by the male clientele. Other women who used the pub without male escorts risked being seen as 'tarts'. In this hostile climate, it is hardly surprising that women's occupation of the 'public' houses was marginal and of a totally different character from that of men. Ironically for them, when they get there they appear to be sharing the same space as so-called 'non-respectable' women. This will not be the last anomaly that will be recorded on women's access to pleasure, as defined in terms of company and alcohol.

It has been the purpose of these first two chapters to set in context and in motion key themes that will recur again when the historical location is shifted from the nineteenth to the twentieth century. I think it will be helpful to identify these themes, derived from the evidence of Victorian history, and in so doing to set out trajectories which will be traced in the 1940s and 1970–80s.

1. A general male bonding at the expense of women.
2. A male 'need' for social, domestic, and sexual 'servicing'.
3. A male retreat from the domestic as expressive of male purchasing power and an ambiguity over men's dependency on women. (This has only been alluded to as yet and will be developed in Chapter 3.)
4. A male ability to purchase 'leisure' and structure its domain, facilitated by male material/ideological domination, i.e. the cult of the macho-drinker compared to the stigma attached to women drinking, being alone or in same-sex groups.
5. The privatized world of women, with femininity identified around ideas of domesticity, nurturance, deference, cleanliness, discretion, and self-regulation. An invisible realm.
6. Female claims to 'respectability' – a problematic and shifting attribution that can be jeopardized by women's actions. Women can be controlled by their being made the subject of such designation.
7. A female struggle to gain access to men, male income, and male social and leisure opportunities.
8. A male resistance to women's demands.

Notes

1 Note also the 1940s' version of this claim in Harrisson (1943:46). This will be discussed in Chapter 3.
2 I have no space fully to detail the 'richness' of Victorian pub culture. I can merely recommend Harrison's works (1971, 1973) as important resources, with the reservations already expressed.
3 For a discussion of the nature and culture of a 1940s taproom, see Chapter 3 on the social ethnography of Mass Observation. Note that the taproom was a male-only room that became a club or games room.
4 For a discussion of working men's views on their 'improved' sexual performance after beer-drinking, see Harrisson (1943).
5 Leonore Davidoff's essay (1976) discusses the moral qualities associated with female home-makers and describes the connection between nineteenth-century domestic life and the contemporaneous 'emphasis on the purity of women and the idea of a double standard in moral affairs' (p. 122).
6 This prefigures my argument that women's presence reminds men of their maleness, with all its negative as well as positive attributes.

Something else than the study of official statistics and the bumps on dead men's livers: masculinism and Mass Observation

Between 1938 and 1940, Tom Harrisson and his pioneering team of 'professional' and 'amateur' observers (Mass Observation) studied the public house cultures of Bolton, Lancashire (Harrisson 1943). 'Worktown', as it is called in their study, was the location for an investigation which aimed to show the pub as 'a living social organism' (p. 340).

This was a radical departure from previous methodology which had been to compile quantitive evidence concerning alcohol abuse, pubs becoming thus categorized under the heading of 'Crime and Delinquency'; problems rather than institutions. It is Mass Observation's serious commitment to seeing pubs as venues for the expression of social relations that provides a fascinating opportunity to 'eavesdrop' on the gender/class ideologies of the 1930s and 1940s. In setting the historical context, Harrisson provides a useful synopsis:

'The last war transformed pub-life. There were drastic restrictions upon the hours during which pubs could be open, drastic increases in the price of drinks (between 1914 and 1921 duty on each barrel of beer rose from 7s 9d to 100s), a considerable weakening of the alcoholic content of beer, a considerable decrease in the amount of beer drunk, and a 600% fall in the number of convictions for drunkenness.'   (Harrisson 1943:12)

It would appear that where the temperance reformers failed, the state had more success in controlling this 'dangerous alliance' of working men and alcohol.

However, despite the depredations of the Excise Department, pubs were the most popular social institution for Worktowners in 1938, after work and home. I am at this point reading 'Worktowners' as male, which is the only reading that Mass Observation encourages. In an interesting perspective on the other comparable social attractions, Harrisson comments:

> 'In six religious sects (five of them new) the ordinary man or woman has also a higher degree of participation, even extending to "speaking in tongues". They are the only other institutions in Worktown which supply a similar participation.'   (Harrisson 1943:17)

It would appear that little has changed since Victorian times:

> 'In a society relatively starved of recreation, working men had to choose the life of the pub and the music hall or the life of the temperance society, mutual improvement society and chapel: there was nowhere else to go.'
> (Harrison 1973:161)

Having spotted one continuity between Victorian working-class life and the lived reality of the 1940s 'Worktowners', I am not claiming that my critical interpretation of *The Pub and the People* will provide a comprehensive historical updating of the evidence. My analysis is offered not as a seamless narrative of women/men and their relations inside public houses from Victorian times to the present day but, of necessity, as a partial and speculative rather than a definitive account. I have, none the less, found remarkably coherent patterns of behaviour that connect the 1840s and the 1940s, and it is towards the social anthropology of Mass Observation that I should now like to focus my remarks.

Principally, the study substantially corroborates the picture of the pub as a male domain. Wives were 'invited' at the weekends to the lounge, the so-called 'best' room. They could also occupy the snug or 'nuggy hole' (identified as the small, private bars in the earlier period). This confinement of the female sex is broken by two exceptions: the barmaid and the prostitute, whose more visible presence is tolerated and partly encouraged, to meet male 'needs'.

To provide something of the texture of the study I shall look at a section on drink servers called 'Beautiful Barmaids', because I think it typifies the complex class and gender patronage underlying Mass Observation's operational ideologies:

'Two young men play quoits with the barmaid, who is, thinks observer, "attractive in a coarse way". She is good at quoits anyway, and wins. One player leaves. She plays again with the other, winning again. This chap, young, red faced, blonde, healthy looking, unshaved, cap on one side of his head, face washed but hands dirty, is apparently on fumbling relations with the barmaid.' (Harrisson 1943:56)

I cannot conceive of another statement that characterizes bourgeois masculinity as perfectly as the above. What is articulated is a complex perspective in which class is both counted and discounted. To put it more graphically – she might be a daughter of the 'workers' but she is after all a woman! 'Attractive in a coarse way'.

This text also hints at the kind of sociological voyeurism endemic in the methodology of Mass Observation and of qualitative sociology generally. The effect of the observer's 'scientific' detachment frequently reduces the observed to the status of objects and this objectification of women is also secured by the ability of the male observers to both share and collude in the male chauvinism of pub cultures that cuts across social class.

I am not saying that the reporters did not 'betray' their male working-class confidants as well,[1] but I am suggesting that the relations *between* men of various classes is the substance of patriarchal male practices which find expression in the discourse of the middle-class editor and his middle-class and working-class respondents. Men of all material positions can tap into the culture of misogyny and I contend that the pub is a prime site of its expression and circulation. I cannot imagine a middle-class woman establishing the same 'rapport' and having access to this pub culture in this way. Indeed, the more I think of it, its very terms are ones of female exclusion and the consequent control of women: a banding together against our disruptive presence. When, for example, Ann Whitehead tried to conduct a participant observation field work exercise in a rural pub, the locals retaliated with physical intimidation, and it was only her 'adoption' by a local as his honorary 'sister' that, as she says, 'proved to be the facilitating formula' (Whitehead 1976:176–79).

In concentrating, as the starting point for my selective reading, on the few high-profile women identified in the Bolton survey, several themes begin to emerge that I will deal with briefly here and enlarge on in the concluding chapter.

We are told from the outset that 'barmaids with sex appeal are a great draw' (Harrisson 1943:56). Their importance in this all-male context might appear an anomaly – after all, we are told time and time again that Bolton men come into pubs to 'get out ow't t' road o' t' wife'. The editor himself concludes that the pub is a place where 'men can meet and talk (out) of the way of their womenfolk' (Harrisson 1943:311).[2]

Why is it, given the uncompromising masculinity of pubs, that the barmaid is an acceptable woman to have in this environment? I would argue that her 'acceptability' is a complex phenomenon. If we think of the popular cultural imagery that attaches itself to the role of a barmaid, we construct an image of a sexually provocative, friendly, sympathetic, and 'mature', experienced woman. Barmen, on the other hand, wear dark suits, bow ties, shake cocktail mixers, and are monstrously efficient. Barmaids do a lot more than serve drinks!

Barmaids are classic token women. A perfect construction of male fantasies – maternal *and* sexual. Mass Observation's contributors document endless examples of the 'pseudo-flirtation' that characterizes the way men interact with female bar staff (Harrisson 1943:63). I would like to generalize from this to propose that this is a 'pseudo-relationship' which is a paradigm of how men would ideally like to handle *all* relationships between themselves and women, or rather that this fantasy developed as the ideal male solution to the negative anxieties triggered in the exercise of male sexual initiatives.[3]

I have been a barmaid and it occurred to me then how the physical layout of some bars sets up a natural 'stage' with the male voyeur in the front stalls. As in a great many other female jobs, solicitous presentability counts for a great deal. Male customers offered to buy me drinks, which I converted to cash to subsidize the appallingly low wages. It is, of course, in the interests of the publican to pay low wages to women bar-staff, who must then rely on their 'charm' to extract money from male customers – a practice that contributes to the publican's profits by creating a 'sociable' atmosphere. An acceptance of a 'drink' thus draws one more and more into the subordinate role, allowing male customers greater access to your time and attention. Being socially 'available' was expected, when a customer had paid for your 'drink'. The job is structured by relations of deference and sexualized servility and, in terms of my understanding of men's capacity to handle relations with the 'opposite sex', it seems to offer men the least trouble. 'My *wife* doesn't understand me.' The classic line reveals implications that the barmaid is a more sympathetic listener than other women, a passively nurturing role that allows men simltaneously to maternalize and sexualize women and thus to render them 'safe'. 'Pseudo-flirtation' is a game that costs men nothing apart from a few drinks yet entitles them to female 'understanding'.

If I move my interpretation of Mass Observation forward from token to taboo, a cultural context emerges in which we can best locate an understanding of pub gender relations. I am using the vocabulary of Harrisson to describe a range of exclusionary social practices concerning women's relationship to the institution; for what was merely read into the preceding account of Victorian social drinking – i.e. female/male segregation – is an established, customary fact in Bolton pub life. Implicitly understood and frequently explicitly designated 'Gentlemen only' areas were found in all the pubs observed. This pertained both to specific bars or rooms inside public houses and to areas within rooms. Taboos operated against women's social behaviour too, as well as against their social location. It was not considered 'respectable' to drink either draught beer or pints. Women as customers had to contend with a range of restrictions that constrained them from using the pub in the way that men did. They were 'invited' somewhat dutifully rather than entering on their own terms, and their unwelcome presence presented men with several difficulties – personal, social, and financial – to which I shall return.

First I would like to describe the gender territories of the pubs and provide some detail about the various rooms.

Vault

Absolutely taboo to women, a space patronized only by working-class men, who, in their various locales, form a loose group. Average consumption per male per night: three to four pints. A typical vault is described thus: 'There is a sawdust strip along the bottom of the bar, or the derived spitoons with sawdust or without' (Harrisson 1943:105). We are also informed that the origin of the term is obscure, though it is thought to refer to an outside lavatory. It is definitely a 'free' social space, where a man is said to be able to 'do almost anything you like . . . short of shitting on the place' (quoted in Harrisson 1943:105). We are informed that it contains no seats and consists principally of a bar counter with beer pumps. What is surprising is that this room offers no respite for men who have been on their feet in humid temperatures for their working day. We are told that it is a place where men come to relax 'mentally' rather than 'physically' (Harrisson 1943:105).[4]

TAPROOM

The taproom is within the same group of rooms as a vault,

though its male customers meet on a more regular basis. A room that offers a variety of games and developed as a games/clubroom, it is out of bounds to women.

Lounge/parlour/'best' room

A room demarcated by its 'trimmings' – comfortable seats, potted plants, tables, and pictures. Beer costs 1 d a pint more in this ambience. We are informed that 'women are *permitted'* (my emphasis). Altogether a more 'feminine' environment. 'And the woman's place in the pub is that part of it which is a home from home, a better home from an ordinary worker's home' (Harrisson 1943:106). In this space, in contradistinction to the lavatory-like architecture/function of the vault, there are no spittoons, no random saliva and dirty ashtrays. Cleanliness and domesticity are the order of the day. A room where men accompany or 'deposit' their wives at the weekend.

Snug/'nuggy' hole/bar parlour

In the larger pubs there has developed a subset of women's rooms which women have 'converted' into their own rooms from lounges. These are areas where women can 'dominate'. They are rooms for women 'regulars' whose seclusion and privacy is ensured by their geographical segregation from the masculine world of the vault. Think of Ena Sharples and Minnie Caldwell in their domain at 'The Rovers Return' in the earlier episodes of *Coronation Street*. Notice that, like the women of the study, they drank bottled beer – milk stout to be precise. What occurs in this space is most revealing. Harrisson (1943:144) comments that 'it becomes a sort of women's room, into which men will only enter in company with their wives'.

This casual observation seems to me quite centrally important, in that it suggests that the sexes are compromised in each others' presence or, to put it more precisely, that relations between the genders are saturated with 'a conscious-ness of sexuality', to quote Ann Whitehead's pertinent term, [5] and it is this sexualization in the context of a relatively volatile social setting that demands various strategic responses and initiatives. As Whitehead remarks (1976:181), 'men and women cannot be non-gender specific friends (e.g. women's friends are always either girl-friends or boy-friends)'. I think it is this mediating reality that principally explains why women customers experience the pub in the way that they do – an experience which I will argue is not confined to the Hereford-shire village.

There are a range of explanations to account for the sex-segregated nature of public-house recreation, some of which I will examine in the concluding chapter. What I want now to propose is the existence of a male initiative that excludes women as a threatening category. I am not suggesting a conspiracy theory, of 'men in dark suits in smoke-filled rooms', though that is not an inaccurate description of a great number of male zones of influence. Indeed, part of my fascination with patriarchal pub relations is with their replication in other areas of life; as Whitehead notes,

'Men's drinking groups occur in senior common rooms, the Houses of Parliament, the Inns of Court, board rooms, recreation clubs, and in pubs, bars and clubs with a variety of clientele, as well as in Fleet Street and Herefordshire.'

(1976:201)

As I have already indicated earlier, in my interpretation of the barmaid–male customer relation, male fear of women's sexuality is a central explanatory core of their interaction inside public houses. Whitehead crystallizes this antagonism as expressed by men towards young married women in the following way:

'As far as the men are concerned, young married (i.e. sexually active) women are desirable potential sexual partners, but they are not available to them. . . . (As a consequence) young married women bear the burden of the danger of potential but illegitimate sexual attraction, associated with double standards in attitudes towards and the practice of non-marital sex.'   (1976:181)

So, once again, women are seen as inciting male desire that cannot be appeased for fear of male retaliation. Men's exclusive rights to women are known to be vulnerable to the 'lusts' of other men. Men are 'other' men too. It is both this insecurity and this dependence that structures male discomfort and power. Brake, contributing to Whitehead's notion of male vulnerability, talks of the generalized sexism that women experience as street politics and suggests that

'the sexist jokes and shouts that girls and women have to put up with daily is an indication of the *complex desire and hatred of that desire* that men have for women.'
(Brake 1980:150; my emphasis)

One way for men to cope with female presence is abuse, another is segregation. To put it more mechanistically, abuse was the strategy used to *ensure* segregation in Bolton pubs in the 1940s – a practice that I hope I have demonstrated is still available to men.

We are told, for example, that when a middle-class trouper

from a visiting company stood at the bar she received 'a certain amount of scorn' (Harrisson 1943:144). It was customary for women to sit at tables and get men to serve them drinks. Compare a modern version of male 'chivalry':

> 'In court Mr Eldred Tabachnik, QC for El Vino's, claimed that standing at the bar of the premises was like being on a rush hour train and women were being spared from "pushing and jostling" by being made to sit at tables. (To which Lord Justice Ormond responded:) "Are you saying it is a sexual characteristic to like being crushed at the bar?" '
>
> (Perera 1982)[6]

There was no doubting the effectiveness of these taboos in Bolton's pub cultures for 'keeping women in their place'. I am not merely suggesting that male harassment works in the *direct* expression of hostility, however, for our oppressions are also secured in the realm of our socially structured perceived 'choices'. On the radio the other day, for example, I heard a woman say that she 'wouldn't be seen dead drinking pints'. The way we live our femininity is intimately connected to the way men live their masculinity in a misogynistic culture. What I am suggesting, therefore, is that male power is not only built upon male practice/female response, it is also sustained by ideologies that demarcate different and usually subordinate social options for women, options that we see and experience as essentially feminine.

In reference to another culture, Shirley Ardener identified two kinds of control operating upon Greek women: the external exercise of prohibitions over movement, speech, and association and the more problematic sanctions of learned, internalized moral taboos. Her study provides a fascinating comparison to Victorian, modern, and contemporary British society. She found that women's spaces were the domestic/ shops/cemeteries and that male spaces were coffee bars and the barbers! Women who were designated 'immoral' were called *tou dromou* – 'of the road' – while virtuous young women were described as *tou spitiou* – 'of the house' (Ardener 1978:68). Ardener's explanation of these phenomena is not dissimilar from the rationale outlined above.

To return from Piraeus to Bolton, Mass Observation found no instances of working-class women breaking the rules over where and what they drank, in the town's *own* pubs. They did, however, record a prime example of a 'right of reversal' witnessed by their subscribers on holiday in Blackpool. Within this holiday culture, several examples of what Harrisson calls 'breakdown behaviour' are recorded. Women are seen to transgress the boundaries and undoubtedly enjoy 'outheroding Herod'. This shocks Mass Observation's moral delicacies far more than the host culture's (Harrisson 1943:249). Women are observed flouting convention, getting drunk, telling raucous, risqué stories, standing at the bars. Harrisson comments:

> 'The girls then tell a number of dirty stories. Observer does not find them very funny or original, but they are some of the dirtiest stories he has heard. *There are no tabooed words whatever.* The girls, the men, and the old ladies, all freely use the odd half dozen common words that at the moment are never printed in England.'   (1943:249)

Almost as if to reassure themselves, the witnesses apparently tracked down the 'deviant' females, who are reported as behaving perfectly 'normally' on their return home.

This is extremely reminiscent of another inversion of norms 'allowed' women in respect of group solidarity, alcohol, and leisure. Diana Leonard (1980), in her investigation into the marital culture of young people, compared the assymmetry of 'stag' and 'hen' parties. A 'hen' party is an 'occasion' when women are permitted to behave in a way that is a diluted version of male peer-group bonding. These two traditional arrangements dramatize the differentiated cultural opportunities of men and women. For, as one young would-be wife commented on her fiancé's evening out: 'They have a "stag party" down there *every* Thursday evening . . . no, it wasn't anything special' (quoted in Leonard 1980:152).

Women's rare all-women occasions were frequently met with suspicion and hostility until explained as a 'hen-party'. As a responsible, heavily pregnant, married woman, Diana Leonard was deemed a suitable chaperon to accompany some parties to a rendevous, thought of as a 'pick-up joint' by the young women's brothers and boyfriends. As Diana Leonard comments, it is precisely this formalized disruption on *one* occasion that ensures the effectiveness of these socially controlling customs. An eruption of female solidarity, pleasure, noise/sexuality/presence on a longer-term basis, with its challenging consequences for the exercise of male power, is a much more problematic possibility. So we can see that the parameters of female sharing and pleasure are very tightly drawn, both in their observation and in their disruption.

I want now to explore how the Victorian practice of 'drinking deeply' was translated and expressed in the gender relations and cultural habits of Bolton's public houses in the 1940s. Earlier in this chapter, I referred to the prevalence of 'taboos' operating against females in these recreational spaces and I want specifically to look at 'why Bolton women can't drink pints' and why Bolton men have to; for part of my understanding of the social relations of recreational drinking is an awareness that male behaviour is measured, too, and that it is not explicable simply as pleasurable power play.

We are told that 'landlords don't serve pints in the parlour!' In Worktown folklore there is a memory of *one* woman who challenged this, a lesbian who, we are informed, would 'rather have a pint than a gill' and who also was noted for the fact that 'She'd stand up at' fire' (Harrisson 1943:185-86). It might just be a feminist whimsy on my part but I noted a sense of admiration as well as censure in the female respondent's views. It is interesting to note how one woman's 'deviance' in sexual terms allowed her to 'deviate' in her choice of drink and physical presence in the pub, too. Was she another token – a token, honorary 'man'?

Nor is this pint-for-a-man-only ethic a piece of Northern exotica. I was once refused a pint in a rural pub (coincidentally, the one that Whitehead studied) and this custom is, I am sure, still to be traced in the pub cultures of Britain. I have also been told of a man not being served a pint in a 'lounge' bar; in that case social-class relations were operating, too. Referring back to my description of male potency, I would suggest that the ideology of the sexually virile breadwinner offers an explanation of why women and men both ideally and in practice drink different drinks.[7]

Maleness is conceived in terms of strength, which is then given as the common-sense explanation as to why *men* dig roads, build houses, construct machinery, and so forth. This ideology of physical superiority is seen as an essential, balancing dominance to women's tender, emotional, and physical vulnerability. Male 'strength', engaged in the manly pursuits of industry, 'needs' replenishing. Beer in quantities tops up the manly body: 'refreshes the parts other beers cannot reach', an advertising jingle which captures precisely the physical *and* sexual undertones. Women on the other hand don't need to 'restore' their 'strength', being weak creatures by nature: what they never have they never miss. This inscription of masculinity also neatly legitimizes male access to leisure and sexuality and inevitably perpetuates the cycle: men 'relax', women remain at home; men are 'bread-winners', women earn 'pin-money', and so on.

Can one imagine a feminist reworking of Bleasdale's *Boys from the Black Stuff* – with a series on how five women coped with the demoralizing and humiliating experience of un-employment? It is inconceivable that women's situation would have evoked the poignancy and political force that Yosser, Chrissie, *et al.* did. Female identity is not located in the 'right to work'. Women, trans-historically and trans-class, have always been deemed as 'unemployed' in the way that their sense of self – who they are – is situated in relation to the categories of married/single, children/no children, beauty/no beauty, and respectability/no respectability. Women's 'virility' is fecundity.

This cosy connection between 'earning your bread' and spending it in company with other men meshes in with the convenient rationalization that beer provides 'plenty of lead in (your) pencil', according to a male drinker in Mass Observation's study (Harrisson 1943:46).

There is a fascinating section on this alleged property of beer in Harrisson's investigations concerning the reasons for beer drinking. An ex-policeman, who appears throughout Mass Observation's study as a most prolific correspondent, inserts the following verbatim account:

'Navvy type of person aged about 35, says "If I get three pints down me I can . . .". (What he said is the sort of thing

considered "unprintable".) It amounted to the fact that
when he went home he was able to have sexual intercourse
with his wife with the maximum of efficiency.'[8]

(Harrisson 1943:46)

There is only one critical break within the whole study on
this issue of men=beer. I quote it in full:

'My reason for drinking beer is to appear tough. I heartily
detest the stuff but what would my pals say if I refused.
They would call me a cissy.'   (1943:42)

Harrisson is sceptical about the genuineness of this statement
but eventually concedes that 'it is probably, on balance, a cry
from the heart'.

If only this invitation had been taken up by the investigators,
what more we could have learned about the male obligation to
be a 'pint man'. Mass Observation does not, however, go into
this. A taboo on investigating masculine practice, in the
process of its construction? In fact, Mass Observation's utility
lies in its transparent deployment of taken-for-granted
conceptions of class and gender-appropriate behaviour, its
critical reflexivity being limited to the transmission of
patriarchal, bourgeois values either through its own observer's
voices or authorial, editorial overview.

A corollary of all this virile masculinism is the need to
ensure its continuance by segregation from femininity.
Despite its claim to be expressive of a 'natural' superiority,
maleness/virility apparently cannot risk the contamination
of femininity. For women to drink pints attacks the notion of
manliness. We are told that 'Worktown' women drink bottled
beer or bottled stout. Might not this need to demarcate the
differences inside pubs, in terms of location, sort, and quantity

of drink/regularity/activities/access and many other gender-differentiated practices, reveal a fairly coherent set of male-initiated social regulations, behaviours that are not specific to this social organism? Mike Brake suggests that this is indeed a conclusion one can draw from Ann Whitehead's work: 'She suggests that these (i.e. cult of masculinism) are a normal feature of heterosexual men in groups' (Brake 1980:150).

Before I close my investigation of the masculinism revealed by and in Mass Observation's *The Pub and the People*, I would like to provide a gloss on the 1940s' version of pub prostitution. I cannot do justice here to the phenomenon as described in the language and mores of the time; I suggest that an interested reader goes to the primary source and conducts a full-scale deconstruction (Harrisson 1943:266–68). What I offer here are a few concluding insights into the subculture within a pub culture.

The first point to make is that the women are never directly interviewed themselves and what we have to deal with are male contributors reporting their conversations with other men. Further, these contributions are edited by a man. The women are thus doubly objectified and kept at arms length, their words and personalities never entering the description. The language of the men reveals more contempt than objective sociology. Thus we find that Bolton's prostitutes are 'tarts' and 'whores': 'The Z who is "well noted for Married Women Type of Importuning"; May X... "can be seduced after two bottles of Guinness" ' (Harrisson 1943:266–68). In one sense, this account of prostitution is a materialist one, constant reference being made to the women's financial position as a factor in their activities. Different categories of prostitution are delineated and these differences are said to reside in the amateur/professional status of the prostitute.

Harrisson gives one vivid account (p. 267) which underlines for me what I alluded to earlier, i.e. that token barmaids and prostitutes occupy positions in pub cultures that are different in kind from that of the 'ordinary' woman customer. Although it is important to restate that the stigma of illicit sexuality can be attributed to *any* woman who appears to break the house-rules.

I cannot help feeling that the contempt shown to the prostitutes arises because the women necessarily have to employ non-feminine social tactics to succeed. They do not merely wait for male attention. The women described have already separated themselves out as 'non-respectable' by being active over the terms on which they will trade their sexuality. A real difficulty I find in formulating this argument is in simply accepting the term 'prostitute' at face value. In a very pertinent sense any active woman, a woman who reverses the normal pattern of male-on-woman predation and who makes explicit the often implicit trade-off that frequently characterizes heterosexual exchange, can be seen as a prostitute. It is as if female trading in the open has to be criminalized/made taboo since it is *too similar* to normal heterosexual relations, not because it is opposed to it. I am not saying that all heterosexual relations are as a consequence reducible to prostitute/client relations. It is, however, in the very nature of a patriarchal society that the power men command gives them as a group greater access to income and resources. Women do 'trade' in their sexuality and 'beauty'. The Miss Worlds and Miss Lovely-legs are not muppets. They are women making 'choices' in this social structure. I do not, incidentally, think that the feminist movement has taken the politics of beauty and fashion seriously enough.

It is this relationship between money and sexuality that

provides a thematic link in the role of barmaid, prostitute, and 'ordinary' woman customer. In their dependence on men, both in a direct and indirect way, all these women share a common subordination. We have seen how this dependent relationship is negotiated by barmaids and prostitutes and I now want to add a depiction of Bolton 'weekend' women into this account. I use this term to describe their presence in the pubs and I want to highlight a few salient examples of their 'bargaining' strategies over this entry into male territory. If I have left the experience of women to the end, this replicates their marginality in Northern pub culture. At any one time they were said to constitute only 16 per cent of the customers (Harrisson 1943).

I have already shown that Victorian working-class women had to contest their men-folk over the allocation of family resources. This struggle finds its expression in another form in 'Worktown'. We have seen that wives who drink 'prefer' the lounge or the 'nuggy hole' and that it was customary for men to monopolize other rooms in the pub. At weekends, however, certain male concessions appear to have been made towards 'sharing' recreation with female partners. But if we look at this 'invitation', in practice we frequently find that women are deposited in 'their' rooms, with men splitting off into the vault or taproom and joining their wives later or re-appearing at 'last-orders'.

The material advantages of this arrangement to men are obvious, for if husband and wife separate a man can drink independently of his spouse and is not required to pay for her drink each time he fills his glass. This segregation conserves 'his' resources. Several men mentioned this underlying material reason for their choice of rooms. One mean-spirited man called 'Thirsty,' with a reputation for being a boozer and a skinflint, would ask the barman to provide the cheapest beer for his wife. She had developed a bargain with the barman that each time her husband sent the money through to the counter, she would 'top it up' from her housekeeping to enable her to buy a more palatable drink. Obviously, therefore, men were involved in subverting the customary expectation that as 'breadwinners' and providers, they were responsible for 'treating' women and this resistance to sharing their money found expression in their insistence on 'going out with the lads'. In all-male groups treating is more equitable – round-buying is something that all men contribute to in turns. Harrisson makes this point quite explicit (I leave the linguistic sexism unedited):

> 'So the pub regular, living at normal work level, cannot be regular with a dame; Saturday night and maybe Sunday night is all he can manage *if he is to have beer on a weeknight.*' (Harrisson 1943:146; my emphasis)

Men's 'regularity' is thus partly due to women's exclusion, containment, and segregation.

I would therefore argue that this important material reason – i.e. a male wish to control a male income, supported by gender ideologies favourable to male but censorious of female drinking, allied to specific social practices of male hostility and violence in the context of a fear of female sexuality and sociability – constructs a more viable account of the institution than the 'common-sense' populism of Mass Observation's crude naturalism.

In concluding this chapter, I hope I have made it clear that 'public' houses have never really been public for women, and that claims to have studied them as social institutions, as living 'social organisms', or whatever, that fail to explain why women have been prevented or discouraged from securing access to them are totally inadequate, as are claims that present women as preferring more domesticated, 'posher' environments. For, as I have tried to show, *ideologies* of appropriate gender behaviour *conceal* rather than *reveal* the power relations that structure this domain.

Notes

1 They did, frequently, reflecting their class and race prejudices. See, for example, the racism of Mass Observation in relation to Irish working men.
2 Note the omission. I don't think the sentence makes sense as originally printed, although it could be taken to indicate men discussing their wives – just as Whitehead found in her study (see page 66).
3 It might seem a bit inflated to construct an elaborate argument concerning male sexuality on the role/cultural symbolism of barmaids but I propose it as a preliminary tactic to open my account with male sexuality at the level of the particular. In proposing male fear of their own power, I am not running into the 'men are oppressed, too' lobby – I just want to indicate a way to understand certain procedures of male practice. George Orwell, in his story, *Shooting an Elephant*, provides a literary representation of what I am struggling to express; i.e. negative concomitants of male power, in this case of a colonial nature.
4 I have a notion, perhaps a fanciful one, that standing up – being prominent – is associated with social dominance and control. I cannot conceive of women leaning on bars in the way that men feel able to do. I believe that their body language has political significance.
5 Whitehead (1976:181) provides an illuminating discussion of why men and women who are not married to one another find coping with each other highly problematic.
6 Compare also what happened to a woman in a short skirt who visited 'The Waggoner' in Herefordshire (Whitehead 1976:176).

7 Obviously, I am not claiming this as true on all occasions for all time. It is a generalization with sufficient truth to stand as a focus for the following discussion on masculinity and economic/physical power.

8 This 'observation' is so multi-layered that it would require a separate chapter all of its own to deconstruct. Suffice it to comment on the gender camaraderie and class discomfort, in tension with each other.

4

A taboo against unbonding, or what the local can tell us about the general

In this final chapter I want to pose the following question: why does 'having a good time' consist for men in their banding together in a misogynistic alliance? I am, therefore, suggesting that the social relations of public houses tell us something about the social construction of masculinity that finds expression in other places too, since misogyny is the ethos of a patriarchal society. Women-hating is no more confined to pubs than pornography is to Soho.

To answer the question, I shall draw upon one other sociological investigation into pub cultures, as my major source: the feminist-inspired work of Ann Whitehead (1976). It is the only full-scale work of which I know that sets out to read the pub culture as expressive of patriarchal marital relations. Mike Brake takes the view, and I agree with him, that her work

'shows how in a rural setting, the pub is used to reinforce the cult of masculinity, women are used to maintain solidarity and ambivalent rivalry between men: jokes were used to stereotype women as contemptible and as sex objects to be controlled, prestige was related to an ability to control one's wife; and that these invariably influence marital relations.'   (Brake 1980:150)

But Whitehead's analysis is not just about the everyday story of country-folk, a sort of *Archers* with alcohol, it is presented as a metaphorical representation of *normal*, male group behaviour. Brake expresses the argument thus: 'She suggests that these (i.e. masculinist practices) are the normal features of heterosexual men in groups' (Brake 1980:150).

It is this two-fold dimension of Whitehead's account that I would like to examine in this chapter, for I think that sufficient evidence has been produced from my interpretation of Brian Harrison's Victorian history and of Tom Harrisson's 'Mass Observations' to concur with Ann Whitehead in her view that the ethnography of a Herefordshire pub is neither perfectly exemplary of an 'ideal type of family structure within the capitalist mode of production' nor 'ethnographic exotica' (Whitehead 1976:200). Instead it can provide us with an extensively detailed study of probable behaviours that women might expect of men in all male groups. What follows is an eclectic commentary on her paper. For those who prefer to go to the source, I cannot recommend her work too highly.

'We come here to have a good time'

In a small rural Herefordshire community, 'The Waggoner' beams as brightly as Oxford Street at Christmas. It is the major social centre, a meeting place for the local labourers who inhabit the settlement.

Hereford itself is a sort of cultural hybrid, being an economy rooted neither in industry nor agriculture. There are still jobs to be had on the land but they mostly take the form of casual, semi-skilled work of a seasonal nature. Large, managed estates are replacing the smaller, family-run rural farmsteads, throwing a rural population into an unfamiliar and undeveloped industrial employment in the 'city' – or, more appropriately, unemployment and rural, therefore invisible, poverty. To some extent, the populace finds itself stranded between two revolutions: the agricultural and the industrial.

It was my impression, after living there for five years, that it finds itself reluctantly adrift in the twentieth century with an inherited feudalism that still structures the deferential social class relations that orchestrate its cultural and political rhythms. Definitely a place where 'Master Phil' would feel at home!

It is also very much a place where it is claimed that men are men and women are women and that the prestige of the former is secured by their successful domination of the latter. Amongst the men at 'The Waggoner', 'drinking in pubs was both ideally and in practice a man's privilege' (Whitehead 1976:175). It is axiomatic in the community that men are entitled to an endless supply of nights out and Whitehead notes that although women are fighting back, their inability to mobilize as a group effectively reduces their initiatives to individual private 'solutions' to a general social disenfranchisement which they all share. There is a concomitant attack on any women who try to 'escape' the home. Even women's bingo evenings are viewed as subversive and it is, therefore, not surprising that women who are seen in 'other places' – i.e. not shopping or visiting the hospital – are subject to rumours of having 'cuckolded' their husbands.[1] This rumour-mongering concerning their sexual 'promiscuity' effectively censures and controls their movements, whilst simultaneously enjoining men to discipline 'their' women more rigorously. No wonder 'running away' features as the most popular female fantasy in the community!

'The Waggoner' is the focus of both male dominance and female subordination. Its ethos demonstrates the sexual antagonism that is embedded in the rural society's gender relations; it is an ethos saturated with male anxiety over female sexuality. Even though women, for the most part, are absent, their 'presence' dominates the discourse, in that the main topic of conversation in the pub is women's sexuality and the effective male control of it. Indeed, participating in 'nights out with the boys' is seen to reveal that they are real men, not under 'her' thumb; power must be seen to be held; 'I came down 'ere to 'ave a drink and a game of dominoes or darts or owt as is going on. I'm not like some buggers henpecked' (Quoted in Harrisson 1943:131).

The geography of the pub is simple. There is a 'bottom' bar and a 'top' bar. Both are predominantly male preserves, though women are invited into the 'top' bar at weekends or on special occasions. Whitehead (1976:175) provides a complete breakdown of the users of 'The Waggoner' in her analysis, but suffice it for me to say at this juncture that *women*'s rights to engage in 'the licensed familiarity of the pub' are very restricted.

The clientele chiefly consists of male, semi-skilled labourers of low social status in comparison to the rest of the parish hierarchy. They occupy the 'bottom' bar and it is here that odd jobs are fixed up in a 'clearing house' where the lines between 'working' and 'drinking' become increasingly blurred (in more ways than one). This particular function of the pub, incidentally, provides a useful rationalization for men's continuous presence.

Generally speaking, in rural Herefordshire the application of licensing laws remains a formal gesture, like compassion to the Conservatives. A 3 a.m. weekend closing time is common.

'The Waggoner' is no exception. The deserved wives of the parish have developed some interesting tactics to subvert the power of the institution over their husband's time and wallets. Several times in the course of her research. Ann Whitehead (1976:199) heard 'rumours' that 'two wives were (said) to have been responsible for a raid by the local police, whom they had summoned anonymously by telephone'. Presumably annoyed by waiting for their men to arrive, these women had taken retaliatory action. Another wife was said to have 'shopped' the local landlord to the police, over his poaching activities, in an attempt at revenge on his late hours and the pub's counter-attractions. Then there were the more direct interventions; one woman was reported to have come into the pub to drag her husband home. Observers said 'She kicked him up the arse as he went through the door. He never even finished his pint' (1976:199). Her direct effort to secure more of her husband's time cost her a beating, though it did prove effective in keeping him out of *that* particular pub for several weeks.

Women's anger at their segregation is also to be found in their organizing extra-parish drinking trips, a focus of great enjoyment and attention for the women concerned. Though I think it must be noted that on the occasion when Ann Whitehead accompanied them, their reception in the 'strange' community was as hostile as it was celebratory (1976:175).[2]

Predictably, such 'adventures' were frequently paid for in vindictively ambiguous ways. One woman, Stella, whose extra-parish drinking outings were a source of male critical comment, suffered a humiliating and frightening sexualized assault (1976:178). This 'teasing' led to her embarrassment at having to explain a 'love-bite', a stigma that provided a message to herself, her husband, and to the community.

Interestingly, Ann Whitehead appears not to link in terms of connection or causality this incident to another public lesson, delivered by Stella's husband this time, to the landlord's quiet, young son and daughter-in-law. The landlord and landlady had gone away on a holiday, leaving the pub in charge of the young, inexperienced couple. Stella's husband took advantage of their occupancy to initiate a series of increasingly vulgar conversations, directed principally at discomforting the young woman. One 'respectable' bachelor commented: 'I was disgusted. She's hardly left school. I know she has two little kiddies, but it's not right. I wouldn't repeat the kinds of things they were saying' (quoted in Whitehead 1976:178).

These intimidations were meant to 'firm up' what the male clique viewed as an effete, insufficiently 'masculine' young man and to 'discipline' the insufficiently subservient daughter-in-law. This interpretation is borne out by the simultaneous production of 'rumours' concerning the young wife's alleged liaison with a workman on her 'walks in the woods'. These sexual innuendoes coincided too neatly for them not to be read as a deliberate attempt to impose normative masculinity and femininity.

Would it be too fanciful to read the 'love bite' and the 'young publicans' incidents as connected at the level of Stella's husband's intentionality, i.e. his wish to offset his loss of face by seeking revenge on a female relative of the landlord, who was after all the original perpetrator of his wife's insult? This might be too neat and simplistic a reading but it is not totally fantastical in the context of a very small parish community (population 500) where bygones are not bygones but the collective cultural memory of a fixed, intense, deeply oppressive, inter-related 'family'. I have already pointed to the fact that it is women's sexuality and the monitoring thereof that are the major sources of inter-male speculation in 'The Waggoner'. At another point in her description, Whitehead comments that 'the social drama consisted of *internal referents* being the content of humour not external, unknown persons' (1976:191; my emphasis).

The retaliatory action of Stella's husband precisely fits both categories that fuel the patriarchal pub culture: male power and male vulnerability. His response was obliquely to give as good as his wife got, in an attempt to regain his credibility as a man, in the eyes of the other males. For it is amongst other men that patriarchal masculinity is celebrated and constructed and it is within this bonding that men also experience their vulnerabilities. Their chief vulnerability lies in their emotional dependence on a desired yet despised gender, a gender group whose sexuality cannot be thought of except in terms of control and exclusive 'ownership'. Thus, a man's failure in masculinity can be provoked simply by a woman's autonomous action or by another man's incursion. Men's reputations derive from controlling women; women's reputations derive from controlling themselves.

Male group cohesion is, therefore, predicated upon being a man's man, i.e. not 'under her thumb'. But this very freedom to enjoy men's company and time-off from the responsibilities of family life allows men a purchase on a deeply ambiguous culture, a culture that brings rewards and penalties. It seems to me that most men are quite prepared to pay the penalties for the rewards of belonging to a 'macho' peer group and that the pleasures of being in the 'master class' more than compensate for the insecurity endemic to male cultures. Whitehead's important insight into the contradictory impulses of the joking/teasing culture of male humour provides some of the evidence for these generalizations. As she herself points out, it is almost impossible to convey the ambience of these inter-male exchanges, which construct a cohesive bonding and an incessant rivalry amongst the men. As the wife of one exasperated customer of the pub remarked:

> 'They teased my husband blind yesterday at the pub. They've been on to him at work as well. It's his own fault – he's a terrible teaser himself. (My husband) came home early last night saying "the buggers will have me walking barefoot yet".'   (Whitehead 1976:193)

It is this ethos that both expresses and partly explains male emotional disablement.

A prerequisite of friendship is the shared exchange of personal information in an atmosphere of equity and trust. What occurs in these pub cultures is the antithesis of friendly, egalitarian openness. Men are on guard, fencing and parrying the linguistic foils, maintaining position, jockeying for position, hitting on the counter-attack. Women can make men vulnerable. In this community, all-women social networks represent a threat to male 'pseudo-relationships'. Women, i.e. their wives, may transmit crucial personal details about men to each other, which may then be used in evidence amongst the husbands to expose an individual's particular sensitivities. Men are therefore hostile to female solidarity and go to considerable lengths to subvert it.[3] They oppose it with a 'taboo against unbonding' which, on closer inspection, is revealed to be a taboo *against* bonding. Male relationships are therefore circumspect, competitive, and transient phenomena. Whitehead understates the case somewhat when she remarks that 'investment in the encounter situation of the pub makes for ambivalence in relations between men. . . .

70

Thus friendships blow hot and cold and men who have been constant companions for some weeks will avoid each other (1976:195).

So we can see that this male practice expressed in pub cultures is a deeply ambiguous strategy. It is male privilege that permits the existence of this particular male 'playground' but it is a playground with swings and roundabouts. Men can find refuge in this space and escape claims on their emotions, time and money made by their wives but it is to women that men are forced to turn for intimacy. Women carry the double burden of being nurturers who have little control over the terms of that intimate transaction. Romantic love is one of the few female-inspired ideologies that has any power in the popular consciousness and our insistence on this as an ideal, even if in practice the realities fail to deliver Mr Right, has to be seen in this light. At least the culture of romance offers a glimpse at a popular shared set of meanings that are female-made. So little in this society is representative of corporate womanhood. There is no equivalent, at the mass level, to male solidarity.

I do not mean to write out of history the women's movement, which is precisely concerned with establishing female group consciousness, but despite its powerful achievements it has not succeeded in sustaining wide-scale mass-mobilizations of women. Sisterhood is at the moment not the equivalent of masculinism, although it is a crucially important opportunity for women to acquire the experience of a shared group consciousness.

It seems to me that femininity is a much more privatized experience than the acquisition of masculinity. Leonard (1980:81), McRobbie and McCabe, and Connell *et.al.* (1981:22, 155) all stress the disruption of girls' cultures by the transition from school to work, a dislocation that young males do not suffer.[4] Their peer groups can so easily become beer groups, sports teams, hobby companions, and so forth. Diana Leonard (1980:87) goes as far as saying that 'women are people with no groups'.

This last point seems to me to bring together the various theoretical and narrative themes of this preliminary critique of masculine practices – namely, that the social construction of masculinity as it is presently defined requires men to identify with their own sex in an equivocal allegiance that excludes, fragments, and abuses the female sex. The pub culture exemplifies these social processes. Think, for example, of the peanut display cards behind the bar counter with their pornographic gimmick – each time you purchase a packet, it is torn off the card to reveal more of a woman's erotically represented body. What a statement about gender relations and the cash nexus – pornography selling peanuts! In this arrangement, providing you 'pays yer money' you can get someone else to set up the opportunity for your own voyeurism.

What I have tried to demonstrate is that the public house is a political institution expressive of deeply held gender ideologies.[5] I do not think that the present trend to 'domesticate' public houses and transform them into more bourgeois environments means that women are welcome. Certainly breweries are concerned by the preference expressed by women for wine bars, in a recently commissioned survey of leisure interests, and we might expect a continuing initiative to 'feminize' pubs and drinking. But the present reality is that women in groups or women alone are still likely to attract the sort of collective hostility that opened this account. In effect, what is shown in the 'local' is replicated in the general; i.e., a sex-segregated social system that delivers differentiated tasks to the respective occupants of that patriarchal arrangement. Public houses, like the other all-male drinking groups cited by Whitehead (1976: 201) – 'senior common rooms, the Houses of Parliament, the Inns of Court, board rooms, recreation clubs – are male monopolies structured by the sexual division of labour and sustained by its legitimizing ideologies.

It follows that we might expect equal access to leisure and paid employment only when the sexual division of labour is finally dismantled. Until then, it might well prove difficult to encourage women to seek political changes that will facilitate their fuller participation in peer group enjoyment and in the economy. One of the obstacles we have to overcome is the model of male peer groups and their oppressive effects. It will necessarily be an uphill struggle to convince ourselves to challenge the sexual division of labour if one of the social rewards conceived of is that of standing in smoke-filled rooms, drinking warm keg beer, drowned in the sounds of canned music and video computer machines.

John Stuart Mill, in characteristic optimism, claimed in 1867 that the excursion (amongst other agencies) had brought men and women together 'for the first time in history (as) really each others' companions' (quoted in Harrison 1971:330). In this study of the politics of gender in a social institution, I hope to have shown that Mill's liberal sentiments find little substantiation in Victorian culture, Northern industrial working-class pub culture in the 1930s to 1940s, nor in the fieldwork undertaken in 1967 by a rural ethnographer. Furthermore, Ann Whitehead's commentary on the rigidly sex-segregated nature of that particular parish still stands as a more accurate view of female/male relations than that of Mill:

'Boys and men do not give up the old pattern of going out with their mates when they are courting, but often reserve special nights – Friday and Saturday – for their girlfriends. They spend the other evenings with their peers, *but once married they do not even reserve Friday and Saturday for their wives.*' (Whitehead 1976:174; my emphasis).

Finally, I hope I have shown that Whitehead's characterization of cross-sex relationships as antagonistic stands as a very useful description of gender politics at the level of the general and of 'the local'.

I would conclude by insisting that one of the most urgent issues to be tackled by men of the Left is to begin to look at their own practices in the light of the massive critical challenge of feminism to this 'antagonism' for, as Lucy Bland persuasively argues,

'Many feminists are unlikely to feel inclined to ally with the male Left until the men have begun to put their own house in order – that is, have started to discuss their own sexuality, sexual behaviour and its effects, rather than leaving the field of sexual morality to feminists or the moral Right.'   (Bland 1985:24)

Notes

1 Compare the notions of *tou dromou* ('of the road', i.e. immoral) and *tou spitiou* ('of the house', i.e. virtuous) cited in Chapter 3 (page 50).
2 Compare this with the 'Worktown' excursions (Harrisson 1943).
3 'Husbands appear to make bargains which often include that their wives should see less or nothing of their girl-friends' (Whitehead 1976:199).
4 We are just beginning to construct a sociology of 'youth' unemploy-

ment, though somewhat irritatingly there is still the tendency to regard 'youth' as male, despite attempts to include the impact on inter-gender relations of such unemployment. See Cohen (1982:43); Gofton and Gofton (1984:280): Willis (1984).

5 Space has not permitted an analysis of Roger Smith's work on Fleet Street pubs (1976) but it, too, describes the economic, social, and cultural capital that men acquire via their easier access to these obligatory haunts of fellow journalists and influential newspapermen. Compare the inordinate struggle that women had to wage to get served at El Vino's bar! (Chapter 3, page 49).

REFERENCES

Ardener, S. (1978) *Defining Females: The Nature of Women in Society*. London: Croom Helm.

Barker, D. and Allen, S. (eds) (1976) *Dependence and Exploitation in Work and Marriage*. London: Longman.

Bland, L. (1985) Sex and Morals: Rearming the Left. *Marxism Today* 29,9:21.

Brake, M. (1980) *The Sociology of Youth Culture and Youth Subcultures*. London: Routledge and Kegan Paul.

Cohen, P. (1982) School for Dole *New Socialist* 3:43–7.

Connell, M., Davis T., McIntosh, S., and Root, M. (1981) Romance and Sexuality: Between the Devil and the Deep Blue Sea? In A. McRobbie and T. McCabe (eds) *Feminism for Girls: An Adventure Story*. London: Routledge and Kegan Paul.

Davidoff, L. (1976) The Rationalization of Housework. In D. Barker and S. Allen (eds) *Dependence and Exploitation in Work and Marriage*. London: Longman.

Douglas, M. (1966) *Purity and Danger: An Analysis of the Concepts of Pollution and Taboo*. London: Routledge and Kegan Paul.

Girouard, M. (1975) *Victorian Pubs*. London: Studio Vista.

Gofton, L. and Gofton, C. (1984) Making Out in Giro City. *New Society* 22 November: 280–82.

Harrison, B. (1971) *Drink and the Victorians: The Temperance Question in England 1815–1872*. London: Faber and Faber.

—— (1973) Pubs. In H. J. Dyos and M. Wolff (eds) *The Victorian City: Images and Realities* (2 vols.). London: Routledge and Kegan Paul.

Harrisson, T. (ed.) (1943) '*Mass Observation*' *The Pub and the People: A Worktown Study*. London: Gollancz.

Hey, V. (1980) Pub Politics. *Spare Rib* 90:54–5.

Leonard, D. (1980) *Sex and Generation: A Study of Courtship and Weddings*. London: Tavistock.

McIntosh, M. (1978) Who Needs Prostitutes? The Ideology of Male Sexual Needs. In C. Smart and B. Smart (eds) *Women, Sexuality and Social Control*. London: Routledge and Kegan Paul.

McRobbie, A. (1980) Settling Accounts with Subcultures. *Screen Education* (Spring) 34: 37–49.

McRobbie, A. and McCabe, T. (eds) (1981) *Feminism for Girls: An Adventure Story*. London: Routledge and Kegan Paul.

Pearson, C. (1982) Some Problems in Talking About Men. Paper presented at BSA conference, Manchester.

Perera, S. (1982) Sour Grapes Verdict at El Vino. *The Guardian*, 9 November.

Rosaldo, M. and Lamphere, L. (eds) (1974) *Woman, Culture and Society*. Stanford, Calif: Stanford University Press.

Smith, R. (1976) Sex and Occupational Role on Fleet Street. In D. Barker and S. Allen (eds) *Dependence and Exploitation in Work and Marriage*. London: Longman.

Stanley, E. (1982) Why Men Oppress Women, or How Experiences of Sexism Can Tell Us Interesting and Useful Things About Women's Oppression and Women's Liberation. Paper presented at BSA conference, Manchester.

Whitehead, A. (1976) Sexual Antagonism in Herefordshire. In D. Barker and S. Allen (eds) *Dependence and Exploitation in Work and Marriage*. London: Longman.

Willis, P. (1984) Youth Unemployment. 1. A New Social State. *New Society* 29 March, 67, 1114: 475–77; 2. Ways of Living. *New Society* 5 April, 67, 1115: 13–15; 3. The Land of Juventus. *New Society* 12 April, 68, 1116: 57–9.

NAME INDEX

SUBJECT INDEX

Note: There are no main references to men or women, as these are ubiquitous throughout the book.

abuse, verbal 6–8, 48, 67–9
advertisements 3–4
agricultural labourers 28
alcoholic content of beer,
    decline in 39
alcoholism/drunkenness of
    women 21, 22, 33, 50
antagonism, sexual 66
aphrodisiac, beer as 28; *see
    also* virility
apolitical inclinations of
    women 20; *see also under*
    group
armed forces 30–2
assault, verbal 67–9 *see also*
    abuse

bachelors and prostitution
    29–32
bar parlour *see* snug
barmaids, 29, 41–4, 55–7, 59n
'battle of sexes' 18–19; *see also*
    conflict
beer: prices 39; qualities of 28,
    39; *see also* draught; pints
Bolton, pubs in *see* 'Worktown'

bonding, male 10, 35; taboo
    against 70; *see also*
    unbonding
'bottom' bar 66

children: numbers of, and
    men's drink expenditure 18;
    in playgrounds 4–5;
    transition from school 71–
    2; transition to adulthood
    28; women's concern with
    10, 20
class relations 14–15, 18, 39,
    42; *see also* middle; working
cleanliness of women 35
conflict 18–19; about control
    of wages 17–18, 57–8
Contagious Diseases Act 32
contamination of women 29
control of wages 17–18, 57–8
control of women 14, 42;
    Greek 49–50, 74n; prestige
    associated with 63, 65–6,
    68–9; territories in pubs
    41, 45–6, 66; *see also*
    sexuality